Footprints

On My Heart

The Unspoken Journey

into Parenth...

By

Chloe Lake

ENCOMPASSING INK PUBLICATIONS

ISBN-13: 978-1-9168921-0-1

In loving memory of my twin brother Jordan, our baby girl Evelyn,
and every wished-for child gone too soon...

Sending love

Chloe Lake

Xx

CONTENTS

ACKNOWLEDGEMENTS

A portion of proceeds from the sale of this book will go towards Tommy's Charity.

Anais Seely for the cover design and illustrations.

Charlotte Turnbull Photography for capturing the 'author photo'.

My husband Patrick for making me smile even on the darkest of days, and our family and friends for all their love and support.

The Seed of Life

You were made up of our very own love-drenched seeds.
These seeds of life were sown.
Letting the course of nature take her lead.
From little acorns, mighty oaks are grown.

My body provides a natural cocoon,
where our beautiful butterfly grows.
The sudden thought of meeting her soon,
gives an excitement only a mother knows.

The red rope of love that connects us both,
with my life and my body I devote,
to keep her safe and fill her with hope,
and in the sand, her name, I wrote.

She shared a sacred space within me,
and rests within my beating heart.
The little acorn on our family tree,
We loved her from the start.

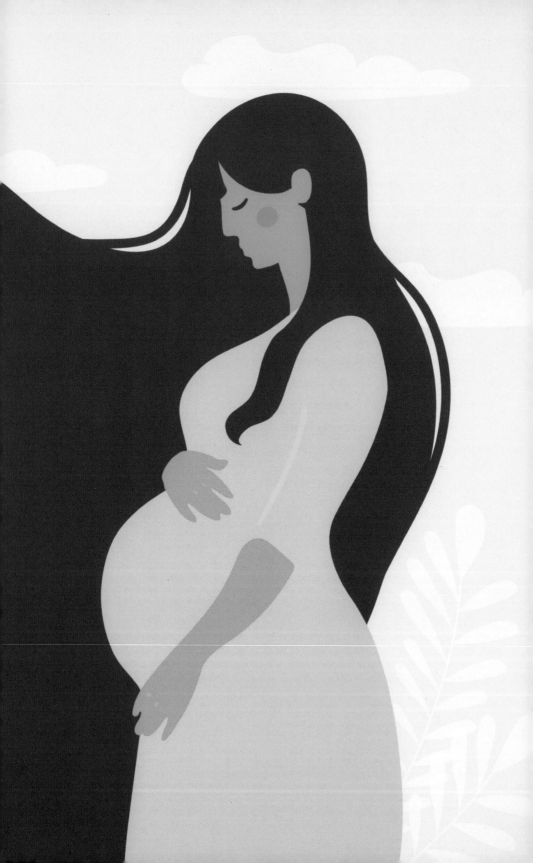

How much do you mean to me?

So how much do you truly mean to me?
You are the very best parts of us both.
Flowing freely as nature's seven seas,
A creation from Aphrodite's oath.
You are the nectar from the Honey Bee,
The pinnacle of love's eternal growth.
You are the apple from the golden tree,
Forever you become a part of me.
DNA combined to a masterpiece,
the most treasured artwork that's come to be.
You will stay within for the 9-month lease,
a little white dove, the message of peace.
Our tiny bud from the red rose of love.
Our shimmering star from the sky above.

One in Four

Two blue lines were all we had,
to show you were right here.
How our world changed in a moment,
and everything felt clear.
All of a sudden,
a rush of emotion,
we planned a future with you.
Those two blue lines meant everything,
all our dreams came true.

You were taken from us,
untimely ripped away.
Our dreams were shattered one by one.
Why could you not stay?
Doctors tried to reassure us,
perhaps an odd genetic flaw?
But that doesn't stop the questioning,
'Why am I the 1 in 4?'

You were our first baby,
we never got to name.
Still looking for our rainbow,
through all the clouds and rain.
But you were our first baby,
we loved you from the start.
Forever our first baby,
Forever in our hearts.

Little Infinity

You arrived in the flood tide of our love,
the missing piece that fit like a pure silk glove.
Somewhere between our hopes and dreams,
you begin your journey down life's infinite stream.
Twisting and turning as you go,
so full of life, as each day you grow.
The birds sound sweetly their perfect lullaby
and the stork keeps you safe as she forever flies.

But the motions change, something went wrong,
the birds stop singing their sweet lullaby song.
The stream stands still, the current has stopped,
winter has arrived and all the leaves have dropped.
The stream freezes over and is covered with snow,
we really aren't sure which way you will go.
As the storm hits, right through my chest,
we try to find peace that you are at rest.
The heavens rain down, they heavily pour
and when the clouds clear, the ice starts to thaw.
The prevailing ebb-tide, pulls you back before time
before I became yours, and you became mine.
You are stolen back to the sea, in which you came,
your infinity was small but will always remain.

The Day the Firebird Flew

The pearlescent echo from four white walls,
the walls which cradled us both.
I remember the physical fight that day,
and how I had broken our oath.
I promised I would keep you safe,
I coloured the once white walls with cries.
I fought so hard to keep you here,
but your life had been selfishly denied.

As the waves of fire crashed through me,
feeding the furnace that burns within,
the phoenix firebird is set free,
and the heavens have their win.
As we welcomed you into our world,
much before your given time.
It was hard to identify which pain was worse,
the heartbreak, or the climb.

The once white room that held us,
now draped with ribbons of red
my blood, my anger, and all our love,
fabricate the tears that we shed.
But fly our little firebird,
aim for the highest high,
take flight our tiny firebird –
the brightest star in our sky.

Forever Missed, But Carried Always

A '**miscarriage**' they said,
the word echoed loudly within my head.
You've got it wrong, you don't understand,
this pregnancy was wanted, and very much planned.
She wasn't a '**mis**carriage' as you say,
the word is wrongly used in every way.

The prefix **MIS** implies a '**mis**take' or error,
I don't need to feel any more guilt or terror.
There's a resultant '**mis**understanding', that the mother did wrong,
making her question every action, now that her baby has gone.
Was it something I did? Was it something I ate?
The questions are consuming and there is no escape.

We might **mis**spell, **mis**read or **mis**behave,
all are faults from decisions we have consciously made.
But there was no conscious thought in losing my child,
I did everything I could, even if only for a while.
I will not let the term **mis**carriage forever **mis**lead,
the loss of my baby – nature's most precious seed.

My baby is missed beyond any measure,
but the memories we have we will always treasure.
I carried her inside me for all of her life,
she never knew danger, hurt, or strife.
I carry my baby forever in my heart,
so that we never have to be apart.
My baby wasn't **miscarried** on that day,
because in reality she passed away.
My baby died, through no fault of my own,
when the angels called her back to their heavenly home.

A Letter to My Sweet Baby

My Sweet Baby,

We never did properly meet, did we? Yet we were together every moment of your life.

I never imagined a day without you, or that I'd live without you for the rest of mine.

It's at times when the house is silent and still, that I think of you most,

when the hole you left in my heart echoes loudly, and I struggle to cope.

It's on occasions like Christmas, and treasured times with our family;

We should have been decorating gingerbreads, and hanging tinsel on the tree.

The grief is overpowering and it can't be ignored,

so I have no other option than to let it all on board.

It's OK to feel sad, and it's OK to miss you.

The feelings are so raw because I loved you so true.

I have tried the very, greatest number of times,

to try and fill the void that you left behind.

But no matter what I do it cannot be filled,

there is no possible way that my heart can be rebuilt.

So I've decided to leave your space in my heart, exactly where it is.

That way a part of you is with me, for as long as I shall live.

It is your space, and I leave it there just for you.

After all the joy and love you gave, it's the least that I could do.

I think of you often, in everything I do,

My Sweet Baby, you will never know the love I have for you.

All My Love Always,

Mummy.

Grief feeds the green-eyed monster

The day I lost you,
I lost part of me too.
There's a 'you'-shaped hole in my heart.
A hole where the green-eyed monster lies,
And tries to tear me apart.

He breathes fire which starts the burn in my chest,
A constant reminder of our empty nest.
The smouldering embers of anger's fire,
endlessly glow dancing with my desire.

The fire spreads fast, and scorns my soul,
I feel I'm beginning to lose all control.
Each pregnancy announcement, and each baby that's born,
Feeds the monster within me, while I'm trying to mourn.

The guilt I feel for how I handle this pain,
Makes me wonder if I will ever be the same,
The same pleasant person I was before,
Before I lost my tiny baby that I most deeply adore.
So while I try to extinguish the fires within me,
Let me cry, let me shout, and just let me be.

My agony isn't personal, I wouldn't wish you this pain,
But I'm jealous you have your baby, when mine couldn't stay.
I'm jealous you don't have a hole, in the middle of your heart,
A hole which is now a monster's home, and is tearing me apart.

Mum's the Word

'Who am I?' I hear myself say.
People don't understand and just walk away.
Am I a mother if my baby's not here?
Can somebody, please, make this clear?

What do you say if your baby has died?
Do you just remain silent? Can we let out a cry?
Is it acceptable to grace people with their name?
And can we talk about them, just the same?
Can we honour our baby from the very start?
Or do we have to hide them within our hearts?

There is no word to identify a grieving mother,
maybe it's due to the abysmal amount that they suffer.
You can identify as a widow, widower or orphan
but the loss of a child is such a misfortune,
that there is no word for a mother, whose child couldn't stay,
so many will brace silence or painfully say:
'I don't have children' or 'no kids yet'
but they walk away feeling full of regret.
Why couldn't I mention my child's name?
Maybe I was saving them from the awkwardness, and of my pain?
'Mum's the word', but I should feel no shame.
In expressing 'I'm a mother' and speaking my child's name.

'It's Just Grief'

'It's just grief,' people say, 'that's all.'
But do you jump into the abyss, or do you fall?
It's never a path people choose to take,
but then again, is the path in life ever straight?
With blind corners, and meandering bends,
drowning in feelings many never comprehend.

The roughest of waters are often uncharted,
miles from the shore in which your journey started.
Each crashing wave pushes you further from what you once knew,
leaving you stranded in the ocean, not knowing what to do.
Should you keep treading water and fight once more?
Or would it just be easier to let yourself fall?

There are moments in life where your world stands still,
grief pauses you in a moment of time, against your will.
Playing the motions over, over, and over:
...repeat.
Reliving the trauma, wishing you could surrender, defeat.

But time and place slowly start to align,
like just after a storm when the sun tries to shine.
Grief isn't gone and should never be ignored,
but each time the waves hit, you remain closer to the shore.
A place where you feel more grounded, and less alone,
A place where both grief and I now call home.

A Child's Game

We fly around the world in paper planes,
and make precious jewels from daisy chains.
We build our cities out of Lego bricks,
and race down the stream of hope, chasing sticks.

Our artwork and memories are drawn out of chalk,
and we use blankets to construct our castles and forts.
Our love is tied up from ribbons and strings,
and promises are made with Haribo rings.

We play fancy dress until we find a costume that fits,
and build the jigsaw of life, with all the missing bits.
We drive our cars on a one-way Scalextric track,
but the boomerang of loss will keep coming back.

Our names are written within the sand,
until the waves come crashing toward the land.
When our existence is then washed away with the tide,
and we are sent to a place where our presence is denied.

We are all temporary pieces on life's board game,
and each path is different, not a single one the same.
One thing's for sure, our time is worth more than treasure,
and if time has taught us anything, it's that 'nothing lasts forever'.

Evelyn

Meaning: 'Wished-for Child'

<u>*(In memory of our little Evelyn)*</u>

Wished for,

In every way.

So loved from the very start,

Holding on to dwindling hope, I

Engraved your name on my heart.

Dimming, tiny candle...

For your flame was fragile and weak.

Our hearts are full of unconditional love,

Raising you was a lifelong dream.

Child, you were our Christmas wish,

How I longed to hold you tight,

I never thought I'd let you go –

Little one – you were prayed for every night,

Dream sweet Evelyn, my darling girl: forever sleep tight.

Walk Through the Seasons

Winter is ending and the snowdrops fall, but
do many notice their presence at all?
They paint the world in the purest of white,
the start of a new year, with new beginnings in sight.

A bluebell's beauty is one many adore,
as their blanket of blue covers the forest floor.
The first sign of colour – the promise of life they bring,
As they signify the inevitable start of spring.

Summer is here and the water lilies bloom,
they come and go far too soon.
They are the image of perfection – a sign of rebirth,
their presence is so striking, much too beautiful for Earth.

The butterflies grace us along with the sun,
their wings silently whisper – a picture second to none.
Their time is brief, before they fly once more,
but we are lucky to have seen their beauty at all.

As the leaves turn golden and begin to float down,
their colours brighten our world before they meet the ground.
The trees lose their leaves, but still stand tall,
so take in the richest colours of the fall.

Winter hits – another year around,
the snowflakes silently fall to the ground.
Each one beautiful, unique and bright,
just like us, not a single one alike.

Snowdrops of Spring

Snowdrops silently rise,

and they softly fall.

But many never notice,

their presence at all.

An image so striking,

a shade of innocence pure.

So picture perfect,

with a comforting allure.

Their blanket of white,

covers the forest floor.

Consider yourself lucky,

to have seen their beauty at all.

The sign of new life,

and promises they bring.

They signify the very,

first start of spring.

They might only live,

for a very short while.

But love isn't measured,

in minutes, metres or miles.

And although like the snowdrop,

you ran out of time.

I will forever be yours,

and you will forever be mine.

Photographs

I hold my love in photographs,
precious moments frozen in time.
your life displayed in black and white,
before the ghostly death bell chimes.

Back in History's black and white days,
you brought vivid colour to me.
I'd seen shades of pink never envisaged before,
as the sun sets over the sea.

Take me back to the black and white days,
the most magical moments of all.
To watch you move, and your flickering heart,
was the calm before the storm.

I now cradle photos of colour,
they are different than before.
You are picture perfect with sleeping eyes,
an image I will forever adore.

Just Maybe

I look in awe at the mother cradling her newborn baby,
her eyes beaming with an infinite love beyond any measure. Maybe –
If she were to escape her new-found paradise, just for a moment,
she would see me break – from the inside out. My shattered pieces torment me.
I'm jealous of their bond, in fact I reek of it... Jealousy.
Why, oh why does she get to have her baby here, and not me?

I wouldn't wish her my pain – I wouldn't wish anyone the agony of losing
a child. It's a pain that leaves you permanently wounded, and the invisible bruising
means that people never see your scars, only your tears... if, you allow them.
Consider yourself honoured to see the tears of a grieving mother, and then,
take a step back – acknowledge her pain for a silent moment – and remind yourself that she
may have empty arms, but her heart is full of so much love, for the rest of eternity.

I look in awe at the mother cradling her newborn baby.
It's like staring through a mirror into a parallel universe. Maybe –
You would have looked like that, a full head of the richest dark hair,
with eyes like honey pools that try to absorb every inch of my face – as you stare –
just before your eyes become too heavy, then close to welcome the sweetest of dreams.
My favourite little could have, should have, and would have been.

The Star of Our Show

Nature calls on us to procreate, but our bodies tell us 'we can't'.

Does that make us a failure in life? Or should we take a different stance?

It's a waste of time to justify why things don't go to plan,

There are certain things in our life, we will never understand.

We are Instinct's puppets. She thoroughly enjoys a show.

The contortionist 'Fate' takes her lead, controlling which way we go.

The Past screams at the Present – scaring her away.

We are forced to live in shadows, for yet another day.

The Future plays Chinese whispers, with Desire, Wishes and Dreams

So everything gets twisted, before the opening scenes.

Love tries to reassure us, we can still be the star of our show,

But Love can soon turn to Grief, if she has nowhere to go.

Grief is often unwelcomed, sharing all her pain and rage,

But Hope shines the spotlight, letting us take centre stage.

Although we have no script, and have forgotten all our lines,

Time takes us to The Future, leaving The Past behind.

Although The Past has gone, Our Instinct is still here,

She always has the final say, The Famous Puppeteer.

We no longer ignore her, and try to welcome her in,

Despite the pain it might cause, Fate will have her win.

We can take a direction, different then we planned,

We'll get to where we need to be if we hold each other's hands.

If 'She' Can, I Can Too

Seasons come and go, they never get lost
but they teach us that it's normal to have loss:

If flowers can die and still blossom again,
then we have to find hope amongst the pain.

If trees can lose their leaves and still stand tall,
then we must find our courage and fight once more.

If the sky can present a rainbow through all the rain,
then have faith that your life will have a colour again.

If after the storm the clouds always clear,
then trust yourself to face your fears.

Daddy's Hurt Too

(Dedicated to my husband, Patrick)

He was right there from the very start,
and my daddy too has a broken heart.
They always ask 'how Mummy is',
forgetting that I was also his.

He might have not carried me like my mum,
but he misses me as much, now that I'm gone.
He doesn't let people see his cries,
he hides his emotions like wearing a disguise.
Although he didn't have any physical pain,
he hurts inside, just the same.

He held Mummy's hand through her exhausted cries,
as I came into their world, and headed straight for the skies.
He praised my mummy for being so strong,
they forget that he was there too – all along.
He held her hand, and wipes her tears,
he walked her through her darkest fears.
He never stopped holding her so very close,
even after the day their hearts both broke.

So when you see my daddy, please ask him the same,
ask if he's alright, and check that he's OK.
My mummy is well, she has lots of support,
but men are very quiet and don't seem to talk.
Mummy was in pain, and there was nothing he could do,
so please just remember that Daddy's hurt too.

The Eloquent Church

The traditional church stands alone,
in the little village, I call my home.
The bell chimes on every hour,
the sound echoes through the old clock tower.
The ice-cold bricks and cement stay strong,
through months, years and winters gone.

But never did I ever, take much notice before,
of the classic cobbled path and arched wooden door.
Of the heavy iron gates that always hang closed,
and the quiet churchyard where the greenest grass grows.
Of the many arched windows full of stained glass,
and the most stunning views, that will always surpass.
Of the way the light beams through all the windows,
and the colours dance off the pews and pulpit below.
Although the stained glass distorts the light from the sun,
there's a uniqueness in this distortion, a beauty second to none.

You being there means everything to me,
and paints my world in rose, as far as the eye can see.
It's shown me a beauty that was never there before,
now the eloquent church stands strong and tall.
In the little village where I keep a piece of my heart,
in the little village where our love first starts.

Next Time...

But what if next time, is the one,
the one that gets to stay.
The one that I can hold so close,
and love in every way.

But what if next time is the same,
the same way it's always gone.
Full of heartbreak and total loss,
the sound of grief's familiar song

But what if next time, is different,
and actually, goes to plan.
My life would be so complete
to hold more than a pregnancy scan.

But what if it all goes wrong,
the same that it's always done.
We would have to battle through all our grief,
If the fight is lost, not won.

We will never know, unless we try,
and battle through all our fears.
The journey's been rough, and it's not over yet –
But we find hope amongst our tears.

Little Wish

I wish on my birthday candle,
and again, on a shooting star,
I wish on dancing dandelion seeds,
and salute the lone magpie flying afar.

I hold hope in the colours of a rainbow,
and in each four-leaf clover that grows.
I hold the bronze penny that winked at me,
and feel peace every time that it snows.

I have faith in the magic of a wishing well,
and feel warmth for every robin I see,
I wish for you, sweet child, every chance that I get,
In hope that one day you will come home with me.

Wishing and hoping is all I can do,
so one day I can hold you close.
You aren't here yet, and have no name,
but you are the person I long for the most.

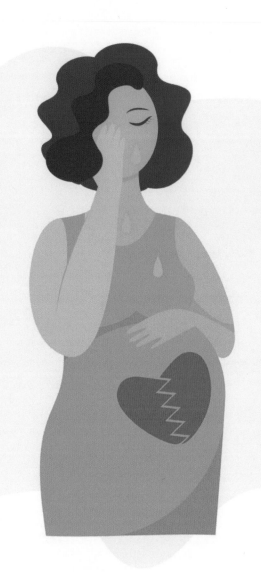

A Recipe for Friendship After Loss

(Dedicated to my very special friends: Ali, and Janet)

A tablespoon of trust
A drop of conversation
A drizzle of unconditional love
And a lot of inspiration.

A teaspoon of empathy
An ounce of everlasting hope
A hint of understanding
And a sprinkle of time they can devote.

A grain or two of inner strength
A splash of heartfelt tears
A slice of roaring laughter
Now stir away the fears.

A gram of perfect patience
A chunk of sound advice
A spoonful of supportiveness
A dollop of being nice.

Stir until well combined
There is no set time to grieve
But wait until you see them rise
Let them take the time they need.

Serve as often as you wish
Follow the recipe above
To create the ultimate friendship dish
from a grieving mother's love.

Light up the Skies

Storms start with torrential rain and sombre skies;
It's like the world has heard our cries.
Thrashings of thunder with electrical lightning,
the build-up of anger can be quite frightening.

But just when we feel like we're struggling to cope,
the clearing of clouds reveals a beacon of hope.
A colourful arc illuminates the sky,
and shows a magical place where bluebirds fly.
Forever rainbow chasing that pot of gold,
discovering the childhood lies we were told.
Finding the light in darkness can be tough,
especially when the journey has been so rough.
But try to remember – when the blanket of darkness covers the day,
the stars will always guide the way.
They graciously glow, and light our universe's skies,
a spectacle of a billion dancing fireflies.
As the sun rises and sets each passing day,
with new beginnings and endings cast our way.
The shadows of our past can hide the light,
but keep your destination within your sights.
Your journey's been long, look how far you have come,
start each day anew, with the rising of the sun.
As you make it through, from dusk to dawn,
remind yourself 'you are emerging from the storm'.

The Rising of the Sun

As the sun slowly rises, rubs its eyes, and peeks just over the hills,

in that moment of peace, silence and total glory, it fills

the earth with such hope and promise, such radiant light.

Yesterday's shadows still loom, but are far out of sight.

The golden beams smile down and warm my face.

Delivering courage, as they lovingly embrace

each person who wakes to face another day,

to start anew, to start afresh, and chase the shadows away.

But with each sunrise, there is a sunset to follow,

darkness draws in with no promise of tomorrow.

So take each day with the rising of the sun,

life is no battle; it can't be lost or won.

But rather a journey that starts way before,

the moments you might remember and so fondly adore.

It's not about the money, the cars, or clothes,

but more about the people we choose to hold close.

It's not about the material things that we choose to own,

it's about the loved ones, and family we get to call our home.

Finally, the sun winks, and lays down out of sight,

inviting the stars to dance through the darkness of the night.

They dance all night within the spotlight of the moon...until,

the sun slowly rises, rubs its eyes, and peeks just over the hills.

2020

What a year 2020 has truly been for all,
Most have loved and lost someone we truly adore.
2020 was the year that everything stopped,
All except the continuous ticking of the clock.
Tick tock... tick tock...
All schools closed, and we were made to stay at home,
And the only contact with others was down the phone.
We kept a 2-metre distance to slow down the spread,
Of this new-found virus that filled us with dread.
We wore face masks in shops, and all other public places
Sanitised and wash our hands to limit future cases.

But the weeks went on and the months went by,
The virus constantly taking life upon life.
The government was worried about our children's education,
Worrying that closing all the schools meant their future was taken.
Schools might have closed, but education didn't cease,
We taught our children the importance of love, hope and peace.
They didn't need maths to work out the equations
Of the virus's destruction and sheer devastation.
They didn't need English to be able to understand,
That there was a pandemic taking over all our lives and our land,

What if the lessons of 2020 were really enough,
To teach our children to persevere when times get tough?
What if remote learning becomes the new teaching norm,
And education as we know it, is outdated and gone?
What if they realise there's more to life than university degrees,
As they have time to play outdoors, and enjoy climbing trees?
What if the fact they were home-schooled wasn't all bad,

And it meant they got to spend more precious time with their mums or dads?

What if this virus, did so much other than just burden, and destroy.

And brought us all a generation who spreads hope, love and joy?

A generation who knows too well, that time, leaves no man behind,

And they also realise, it doesn't cost a penny, to be kind,

They never take for granted what we all did before,

The once simple things in life we all now treasure and adore,

A warm embrace, a loving hug, but a year spent apart,

The year of 2020 will be engraved on all our hearts.

There is no footprint too small

that it cannot leave

an imprint on this world

IN LOVING MEMORY OF:

Josh Northcott

LO (Little One) Bampton-Hoare

Julie Howard

Jordan Lott

Nano Bean

Robson Charles Huxtable

Matilda Butt Redden

Robin Nathaniel Nordmark

Tarquin Martin

The Two Little Horaces

Alex Culver Pyke

A & a Rushton Babies

Kieron Beer

Nevaeh Kaminski

Peppercorn

Eleana Rose Rudkin

Bailey Eavis

Harley Matthew Ball

The Littlest Lake Babies

Evelyn Lake

...And every child gone too soon

My personal connection to 'baby loss' stems right back from birth. My twin brother Jordan and I were born 3 months prematurely in 1996. Sadly, due to our premature birth, Jordan passed away at 11 days old.

Despite defying all odds, I truly count my blessings every day, and know I am very lucky to be here. The loss of my brother has definitely been a driving force throughout my life; maybe it's because in some ways I feel like I'm living for both of us?

In 2017, at the age of 21, I graduated Plymouth University with BSc (Hons) in Tourism Management. I went into work straight out of university, and started my first full-time job as a Teaching Assistant at a local secondary school. I fell in love with my job role, and I've been there ever since.

I was lucky enough to marry my best friend in 2018, and we immediately decided that we wanted to start a family of our own. Little did we know at the time, the journey we were about to face... In July 2020, I ended up losing my 4th consecutive pregnancy, my daughter Evelyn, during the second trimester.

So, by 24, I'm a mum of 4, and although you can't see my children, I get to carry them in my heart instead. People rarely talk about the grief, devastation and heartbreak after losing a baby. Therefore, as a way of coping and connecting with my feelings, I started to write poetry. Which has hereby resulted in the creation of *Footprints On My Heart.*

Printed in Great Britain
by Amazon

85541841R00027